EARRING DESIGNS BY SIG

BOOK II

WRITTEN & ILLUSTRATED BY

SIGRID WYNNE-EVANS

Eagle's View Publishing
A WestWind, Inc. Company
6756 North Fork Road
Liberty, UT 84310

Library of Congress Number: 93-70576
ISBN 0-943604-39-7

First Edition

15 14 13 12 11 10 9 8 7 6 5 4 3 2 1

TABLE OF CONTENTS

TABLE OF CONTENTS (Continued)

ABOUT THE AUTHOR

Sig has been beading for about ten years and teaching beadwork for the past four. She is the author of two books and is working on a third at present. If you would like to write to her with comments on her work or ideas for other books, simply write to "Sig % Eagle's View Publishing Company, 6756 North Fork Road, Liberty, UT 84310. She is always interested in hearing from her readers.

INTRODUCTION

Most of the designs in this book are made using seed beads, but bugle beads, small 4mm crystals and other beads may be used on the dangles for accents. Seed beads come in different sizes such as 9/°, 10/°, 11/°, 12/°, 13/°, 14/°, 15/° and 16/° (the higher the number, the smaller the bead). Of these sizes, 11/° is the most widely used as it is available in more colors and styles. An approximate gauge is listed below:

$$11/° - 17 \text{ beads per inch}$$
$$12/° - 19 \text{ beads per inch}$$
$$13/° - 21 \text{ beads per inch}$$
$$14/° - 23 \text{ beads per inch}$$

When working the designs in this book, bead size uniformity is of the utmost importance. Care must be taken in choosing the beads that will be used!

The number one rule when buying beads is to buy all of the beads needed of the style and color that will be used to complete each project, and if a certain color or style is favored, it is best to buy in quantity. Bead dye batches vary in shade, it is possible to forget where beads were purchased and styles are sometimes discontinued.

Beads may be purchased in several ways. They come in nice little packages of 1/2 Oz or 1 Oz., in tubes, loose or in hanks. If purchased in Indian craft supply houses, they usually come in hanks which are strings of beads from Czechoslovakia. When buying in bulk, hanks are available in kilos (2.2 pounds), half kilos and quarter kilos. These beads are generally fairly uniform but even these beads should be individually selected carefully for use with the designs in this book.

Bead styles vary greatly and it is possible to use most of them with these designs. Smooth beads have been tumbled giving the surface a regular texture. Cut beads can be found as 2-cuts, 3-cuts and hex-cuts. Charlotte beads have little facets cut into them on 1 or 2 sides; these beads reflect light nicely and lend a project a very elegant look.

Seed beads also come in a variety of finishes. Aurora Borealis (AB) beads have a rainbow effect on the surface; these are also known as Iris, Iridescent or Fire Polish. Ceylon beads have a surface that is somewhat pearlized. An old-time finish that is opaque, but with a great deal of depth, is known as Greasy. The most common, of course, is opaque and light will not pass through these beads; they are sometimes referred to as chalky colors. Transparent beads allow the light to pass through, giving an earring a stained glass appearance.

There are also a number of styles that should not be used: Metallic beads are very attractive, but the sun will fade them and the metallic finish will rub off. Surface dyed beads will also fade. A way to spot this variety is a mottled appearance on the surface of the bead (an uneven color) or holes that are just a bit darker in shade than the surface of the bead. Color-lined beads can also be a problem as the inside color may rub off and will also fade.

The best beading needles are manufactured in England. A size 13/0 beading needle will work well with a size 11/° seed bead. If smaller beads are used, a size 15/0 or 16/0 needle is suggested. Actually the smallest needle possible that will pass through beads more than once is best.

Thread is very important. Do Not use regular cotton or cotton/polyester sewing thread. Beading thread, or Nymo (made of nylon), is best for beading. It is strong and durable and will not fray. The recommended sizes are "A", "0" or "00". Nymo does have a tendency to stretch, so give it a good stretch before using to help prevent the dangles from becoming loose.

The work space used can be as important as the materials. Every beader has their own preference, but there are certain necessities that are common to all. A great deal of physical pain in the back, shoulders, neck and wrist can be avoided with proper posture and position. Ample space is needed to insure freedom of movement and to make sure that threads do not get caught on items crammed into a tiny work space.

It's a good idea to find a desk or table and chair that is comfortable and to claim this area as the work space. It will be easier to focus and the beading will go faster and better than if a different area is used each time.

Lighting is another important consideration. Good lighting makes it possible to see the true color of the beads, to thread the small beading needles and to do quality work. A 75 or 100 watt bulb works well but stay away from fluorescent lighting as this kind of light does not show the real color of the beads and seems to cause eye fatigue. To help see better it is possible to use magnifying glasses. The type that is available for embroidery at needle shops works well as do jewelers' magnifying glasses.

Having the beads organized will help the work go faster. Flat, multi-compartment boxes are good for large beads, but are not recommended for seed beads; it is difficult to get the beads out of those deep compartments. Some people use small plastic jars that screw into each other and these work fairly well, but have a tendency to come apart and scatter beads.

Baby food jars work fairly well for bead storage as it is possible to pour the beads into the lids and work from the lid, it is easy to keep the colors separate with them and the jars are clear so that colors can be identified easily. The disadvantages are that the sizes of these jars are limited, they are not very compact and they break in transport.

The method that works best for the author is using small plastic boxes with snap-on lids. These are compact, they do not break and are available in several sizes; one size is just right for a hank, larger ones for greater quantities. The disadvantages are that they can pop open and, because of the milky color of the plastic, it is sometimes necessary to open them to make sure of the color.

All of the above is important to the concept of design: (1) The single most important step in working with the designs in this book is using beads that are uniform in size. Some of these designs have the flow of a line through them. If the beads used vary too much in size or shape the line will be crooked or have breaks in it. Be careful not to let the bead size vary too much. (2) The use of color is very important. Even though the colors are charted, attention must be given to contrast. If a very pale pink is used next to a very pale amethyst, the design could get "lost" as the colors will tend to blend together. (3) Mixing of transparent and opaque beads must be done with caution. If transparent beads are used for the background and opaque beads for the design, the design will stand out beautifully. However, if transparent beads are used in the outline of a design (especially the lighter colors), the lines will be lost. Always try to use colors that will contrast strongly instead of those that are close in hue.

THOUGHTS ON THE BEADWORK BUSINESS

Any craft business is difficult but beadwork is perhaps harder than most as, on a per hour basis, the returns are minimal. Beadwork, as a rule, is an under-valued art. Many chain stores sell beadwork that is made in third world countries where beaders make but pennies a day. There are domestic companies that systematically "rip off" the naive beadworker. And then, of course, there is the "Aunt Suzy" beader, who will make earrings for next to nothing, if she charges anything at all.

As a beader who wishes to sell beadwork as Art and for profit, it is extremely difficult to compete with any of the above. People look at beads as inexpensive material and as a craft that is easily learned. True, seed beads are relatively inexpensive and the basics of the craft are not difficult to learn. But, in order to do it well, it takes patience, time and some degree of talent.

The following is a simplified formula for pricing that is used by many craftspeople. *Price = (cost of materials x 3) + $ amount per hour.* If a pair of earrings sell at retail for $40.00 and take six hours to create, the craftsperson makes about $6.00 per hour. This is without factoring in the cost of the materials and all of the other expenses involved (gas, travel, ads, etc.). It is easy to see that few beaders will become rich selling their creations and that the enjoyment of the Art must be part of the motivation.

Still the Art form deserves to be recognized and the best way for this to happen is to tell people about the effort that it takes to do the work and to sell the work at a price that is representative of the effort necessary to create the work.

There are a number of places to sell earrings. Small fairs,

swap meets, flea markets and church bazaars usually do not work out as people are looking for bargains and not quality art. On the other hand, Art Festivals work well because they are well promoted, well attended and the clientele is looking for "something different." Still, these are sometimes expensive to attend and expenses have to be factored into the selling price. Check these shows out before making a commitment.

Selling to retail stores is a possiblity, but in order to do so it will be necessary to" wholesale" the earrings. That means that if a pair of earrings retails for $40.00, a store will expect to buy it for $20.00; many "specialty stores" will need to sell them for even more. Another manner of dealing with stores is consignment.

Consignment means leaving the merchandise with the retail store and getting paid for it only after the earrings are sold; the craftsman's percentage from the sale can be anywhere from 50% to 80% of the retail selling price. In any event, if consignment is to be the working agreement, make sure everything is agreed to in writing. The agreement should outline what percentage the store will keep, how and when payment will be made, who is responsible for any theft and damage, how the merchandise will be displayed, whether the craftsperson is responsible for any part of promotion or ads, and the time period of the agreement.

Exclusivity is also important when working with retail outlets. Just as it may be a good idea to agree not to offer your earrings to the retail outlet's competition, the store should agree not to try to sell your competition's creations, etc.

The designs in this book are examples of some of the beautiful work that can be created with seed beads. For more, please see **Book I** in the *Earring Designs by Sig* series.

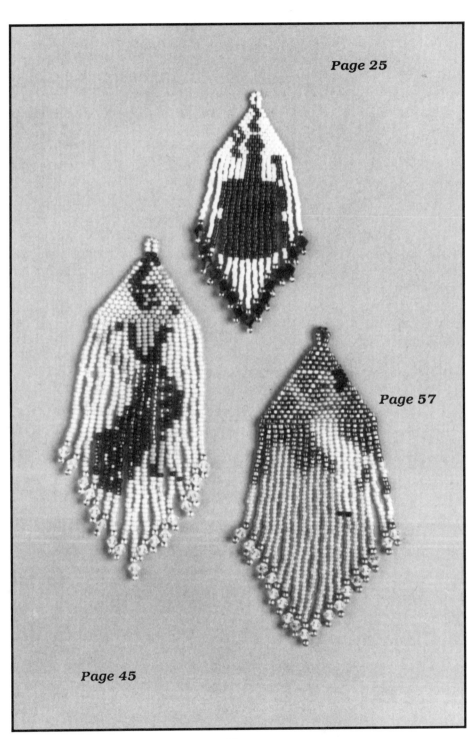

Page 25

Page 57

Page 45

EARRING DESIGNS BY SIG

The earrings in this book are of two types - the *Diamond* and the *Triangle*. Both are done using the Comanche Weave (sometimes called the Brick Stitch, Bedouin Stitch, Apache Weave, etc.). It is strongly recommended that if the craftsperson is unfamiliar with this technique, the base row should be practiced until it is comfortable, perhaps using bugle beads. Even though these designs use seed beads in the base row, there is no difference in the technique; an understanding of how much tension is needed as well as a good deal of dexterity in the fingertips must be developed. It is much easier to learn how to do the base row with bugles and will be less frustrating in the beginning.

These creations are done in three parts: The Base Row, the Top and the Dangles. The Base Row is the widest row of the earring. It is best to start with about 36" of thread (see the *Introduction* for some ideas on thread and needles). The use of bees wax on the thread is up to the individual craftsperson: It can help keep the thread from tangling and fraying, but it can also add bulk to the thread and give a waxy build-up on the tops of the beads.

THE BASE ROW

Begin the earring by forming the Base Row. As shown in the illustrations (*Figure 1*), place two beads on the thread and push

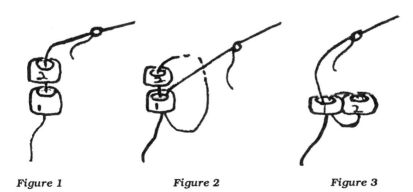

| Figure 1 | Figure 2 | Figure 3 |

them to about 6-8" from the end. Holding the short thread, make a clockwise circle with the needle and go up through the first seed bead (*Figure 2*). Pull the thread tight and the two beads will come together side by side as shown in *Figure 3*. The needle is now coming up through the first bead and this step is finished by taking the needle down through the second seed bead (*Figure 4*).

Figure 4

Hold these two beads close together with the thumb and index finger and make sure that the thread is tight. Pick up one bead with the needle, placing it next to bead number 2 and the thread will be coming up out of bead number 3. Go back down into bead number 2, then up through bead number 3 and pull the thread taut (*Figures 5 & 6*).

Figure 5   Figure 6

Now, with the thread coming up out of bead number 3, pick up another bead and add this to the Base Row as shown in *Figures 7 & 8*. As can easily be seen, there is a pattern emerging. The needle and thread are following a circular motion. Always follow the direction of the thread and continue in this manner until all of the required number of beads have been added to the Base Row.

<table>
<tr><td>Figure 7</td><td>Figure 8</td></tr>
</table>

If there is an odd number of beads in the Base Row, the needle will be coming out of the top of the last bead. If the Base Row has an even number of beads, work the thread through the beads so that it is coming out of the top as shown in *Figure 9.*

Figure 9

THE TOP

With the needle and thread coming up through the last bead in the row, add a bead and then bring the needle under the threads

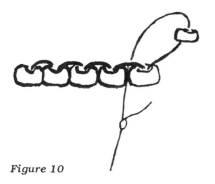 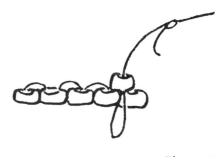

Figure 10

Figure 11

that connect the two beads in the base row. Pull the thread tight. Now bring the needle and thread up through the added bead and continue in this manner until the row above the Base Row is completed (See *Figures 10* and *11*). To add the next row up, simply follow this procedure back the other way. Continue adding rows (each row will be decreased by one bead) until the top row has two beads in it.

To add the earwire loop, add six beads once the last row is complete. Bring the needle and thread through the six beads and the two beads in the last row in a circular fashion (*Figure 12*). Go back through these eight beads several times for strength.

Figure 12

Work the needle and thread down through the top portion until the end of the Base Row is reached. If this is a Triangle Design Earring, it is time to add the Dangles (Figure 13). If this is a Diamond Design Earring, turn the work upside down and do the

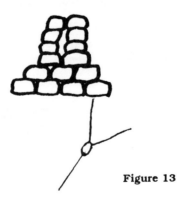

Figure 13

work again as described above (except for the earring loop). At this stage, place a needle on the 6-8" end thread and work it into the earring.

THE DANGLES

Dangles for the triangle-shaped earrings are easy. Read the chart vertically and put on all of the beads in the vertical row along with any accent beads such as bugles and/or crystals. Do Not hesitate to be creative and add a personal touch to these patterns. Once all of the beads are in place, go back up through the beads again, as well as the Base Row bead, and go through the next bead to add the next dangle. At least one bead at the end of the dangle (an anchor) must be used to hold the others in place (*Figure 14*). Three beads may be used as the anchor and this will form a nice little "flower" (*Figure 15*).

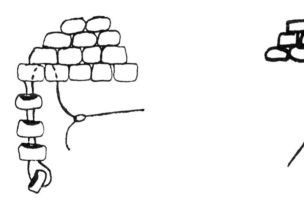

Figure 14   *Figure 15*

For the diamond earrings there are two ways to add the dangles. One is to add dangles in the same manner as with the triangle motif (See *Figure 16*, next page). Note that a dangle will come down out of every other row.

Another technique is to make loops. Again, this will involve every other row. Please note that the portion of the loop that is on the lower row will have two beads less; this is to compensate for the shorter distance traveled by the inside beads of the dangle as illustrated in *Figure 17*.

Figure 16   *Figure 17*

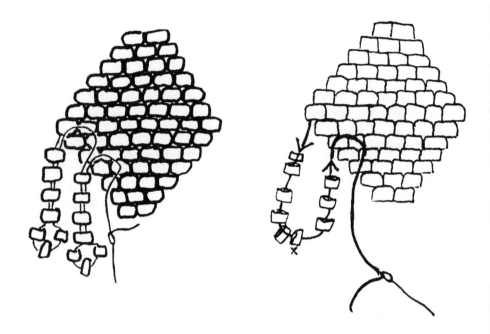

FINISHING

To finish the earring, bring the needle and thread out of the top portion of the earring. A simple, small knot on the edge of the earring will end the work. It is a good idea to melt the Nymo after the knot is made, but extreme care must be taken not to melt other threads. The advantage of melting the thread is that it helps to keep the end from pulling through as it adheres to itself. Adding thread when needed, while making the earring, is done in the same manner. If the white Nymo shows too much on the edges, it is possible to use a felt tipped pen to color the thread.

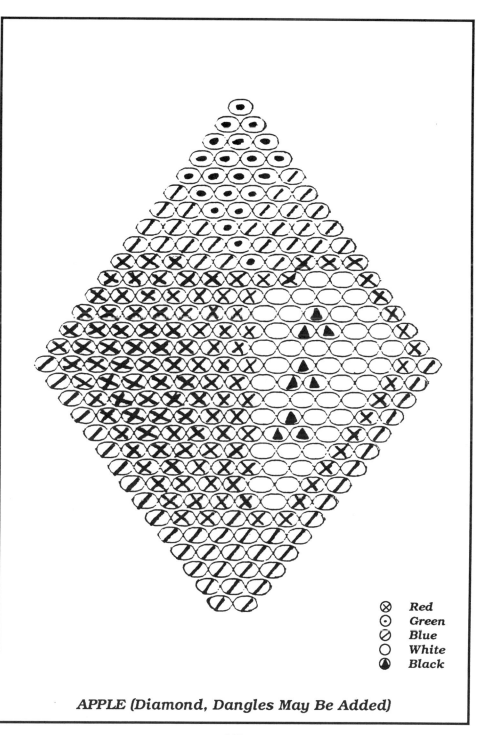

⊗	Red
⊙	Green
⊘	Blue
○	White
◑	Black

APPLE (Diamond, Dangles May Be Added)

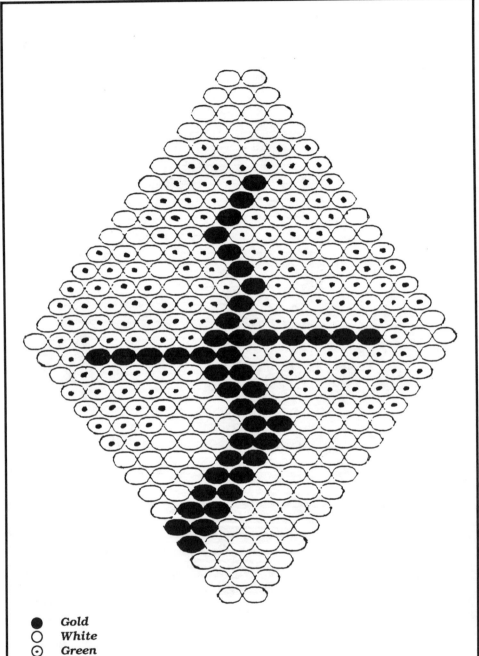

● Gold
○ White
⊙ Green

SHAMROCK (Diamond - Dangles May Be Added)

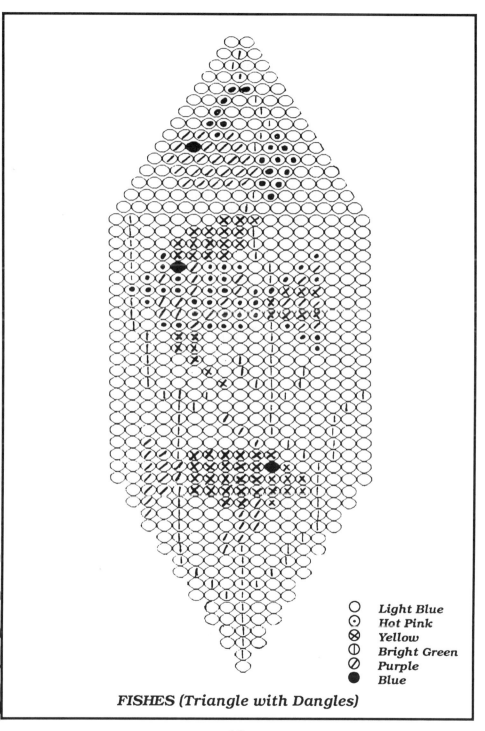

FISHES (Triangle with Dangles)

	Light Blue
⊙	Hot Pink
⊗	Yellow
⦶	Bright Green
⊘	Purple
●	Blue

19

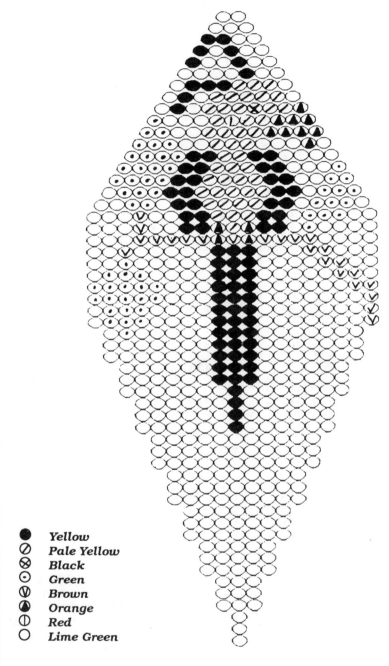

Legend:

- ● Yellow
- ⊘ Pale Yellow
- ⊗ Black
- ⊙ Green
- Ⓥ Brown
- ◖ Orange
- ⦶ Red
- ○ Lime Green

COCKATIEL (Triangle with Dangles)

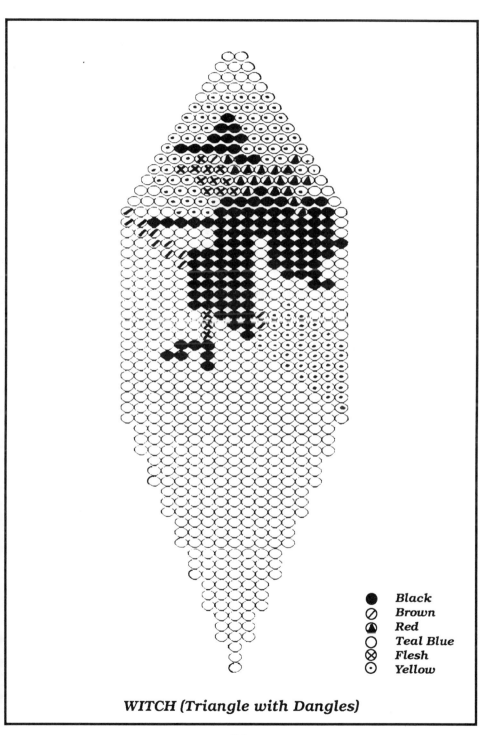

●	Black
⊘	Brown
◓	Red
○	Teal Blue
⊗	Flesh
⊙	Yellow

WITCH (Triangle with Dangles)

21

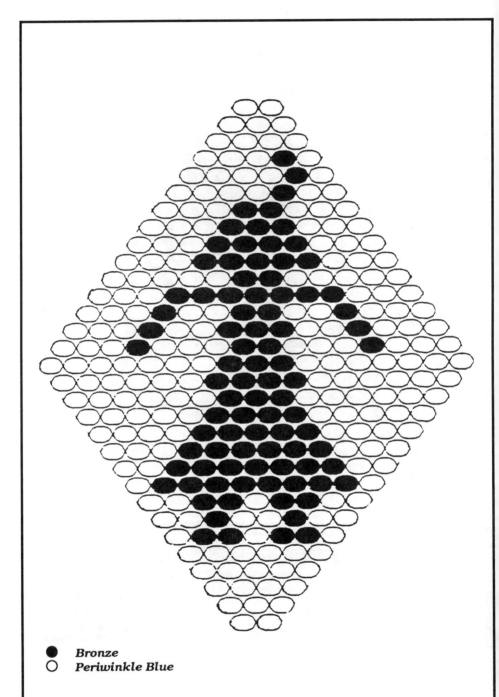

Bronze
Periwinkle Blue

KACHINA (Diamond - Dangles May Be Added)

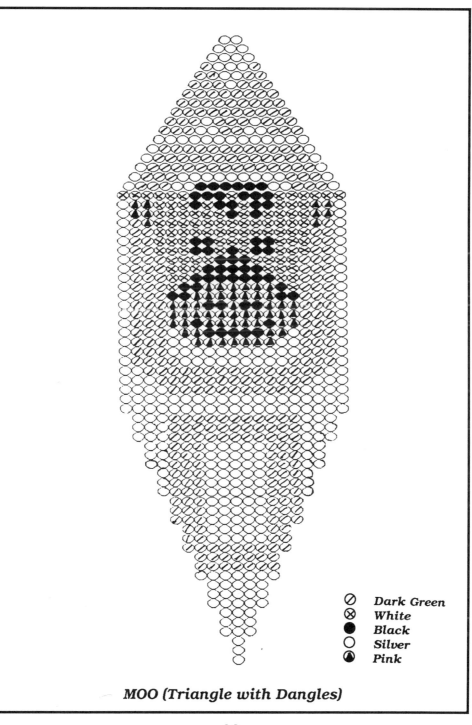

MOO (Triangle with Dangles)

Legend:
- ⊘ Dark Green
- ⊗ White
- ● Black
- ○ Silver
- ◑ Pink

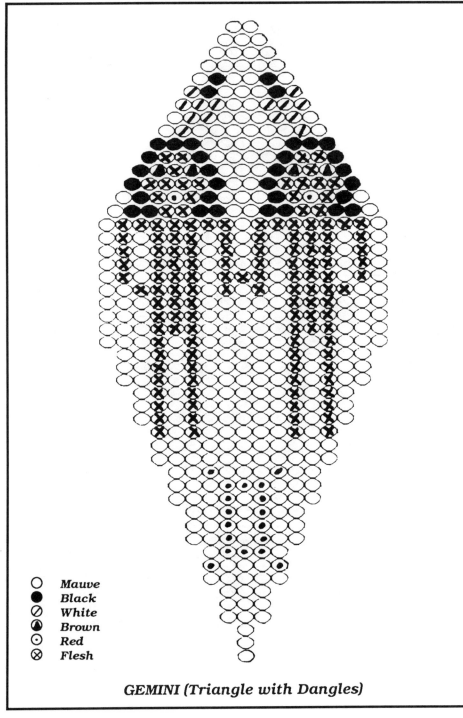

○	Mauve
●	Black
⊘	White
◑	Brown
⊙	Red
⊗	Flesh

GEMINI (Triangle with Dangles)

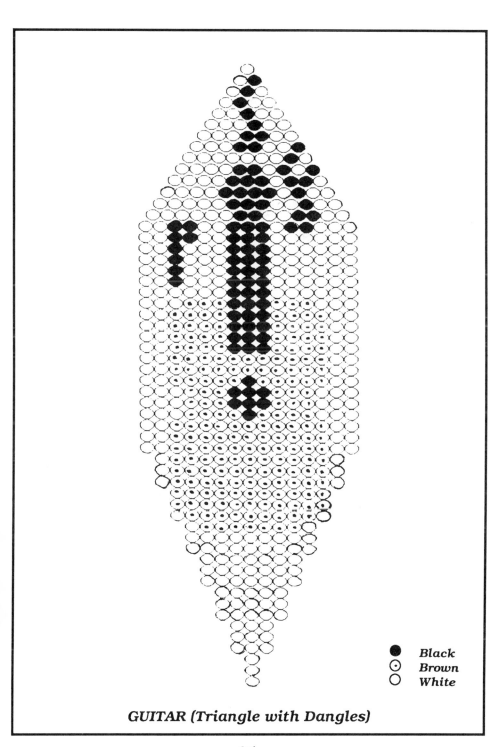

GUITAR (Triangle with Dangles)

25

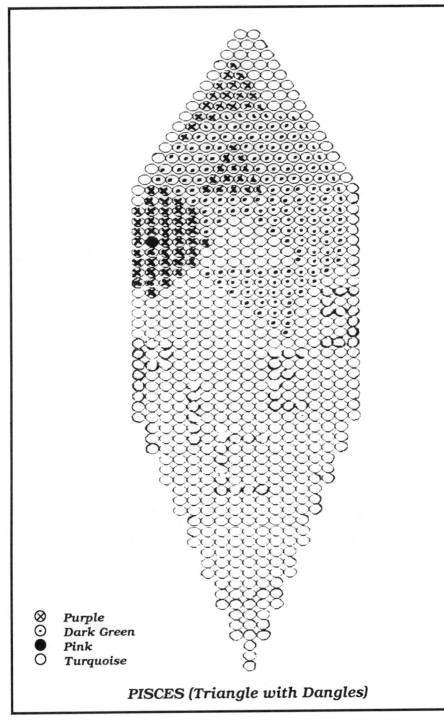

⊗ Purple
⊙ Dark Green
● Pink
○ Turquoise

PISCES (Triangle with Dangles)

26

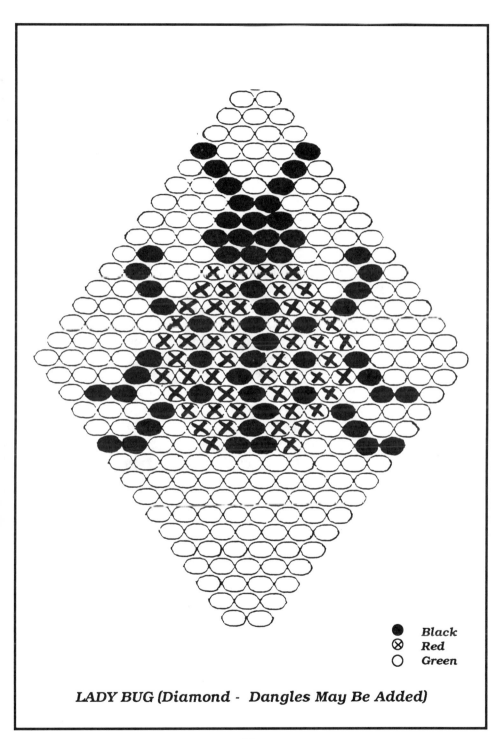

LADY BUG (Diamond - Dangles May Be Added)

27

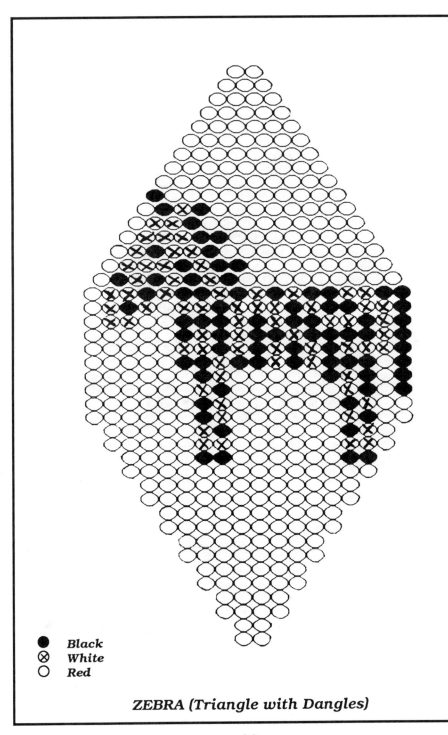

○   **Black**
⊗   **White**
○   **Red**

ZEBRA (Triangle with Dangles)

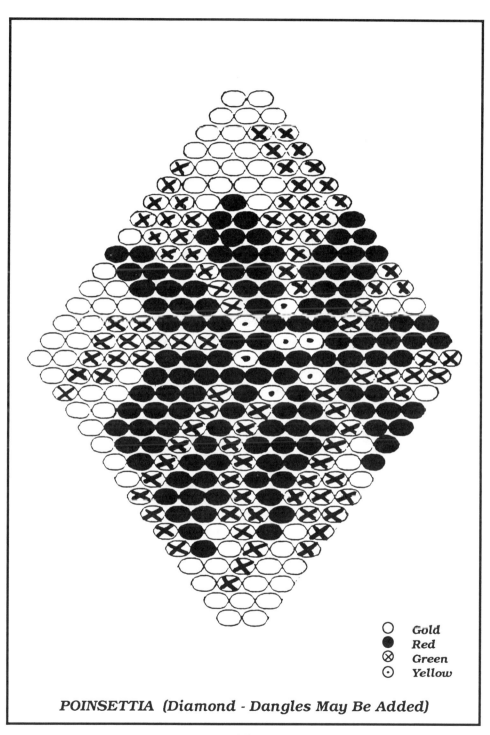

○	Gold
●	Red
⊗	Green
⊙	Yellow

POINSETTIA (Diamond - Dangles May Be Added)

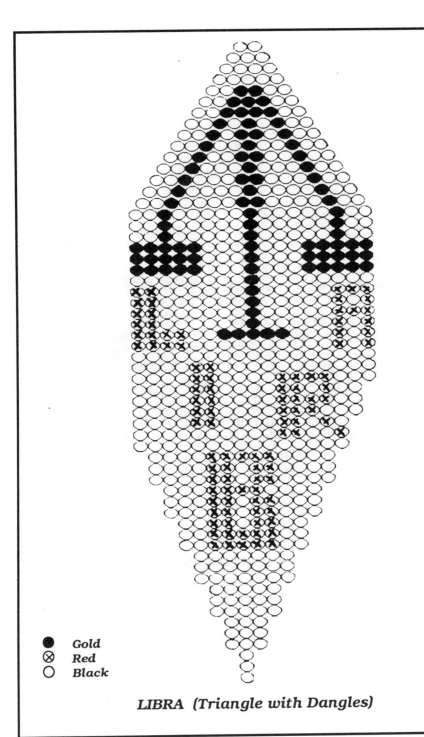

LIBRA *(Triangle with Dangles)*

Gold
Red
Black

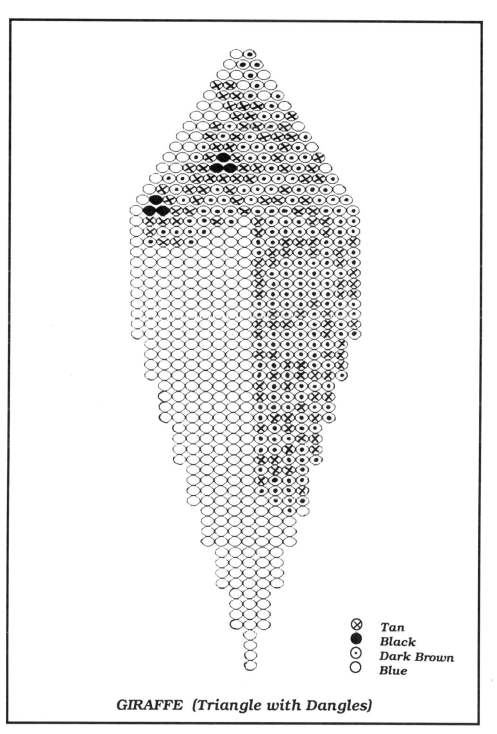

⊗	Tan
●	Black
⊙	Dark Brown
○	Blue

GIRAFFE (Triangle with Dangles)

31

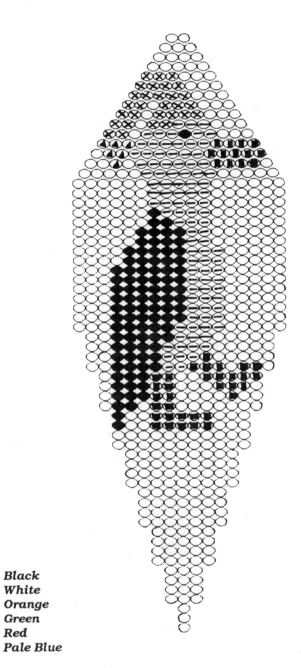

Black
White
Orange
Green
Red
Pale Blue

SEAGULL *(Triangle With Dangles)*

Page 17

Page 18

Page 19

Page 20

PLATE I

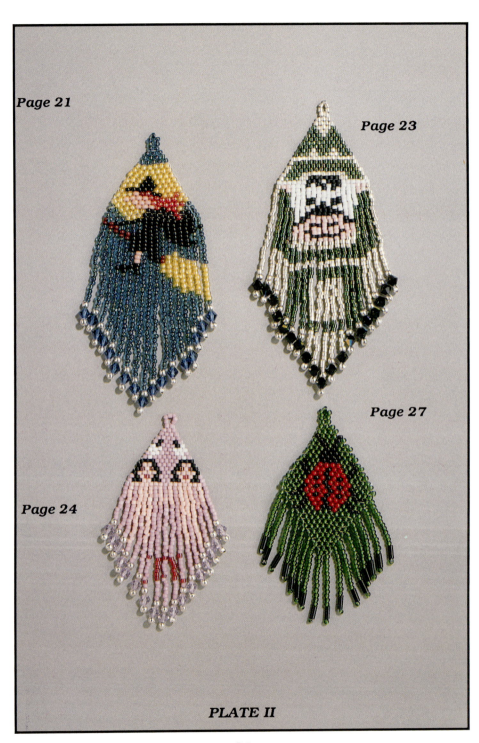

Page 21

Page 23

Page 27

Page 24

PLATE II

34

Page 28

Page 29

Page 30

Page 31

PLATE III

Page 32

Page 42

Page 43

Page 44

PLATE IV

36

Page 46

Page 47

Page 48

Page 49

PLATE V

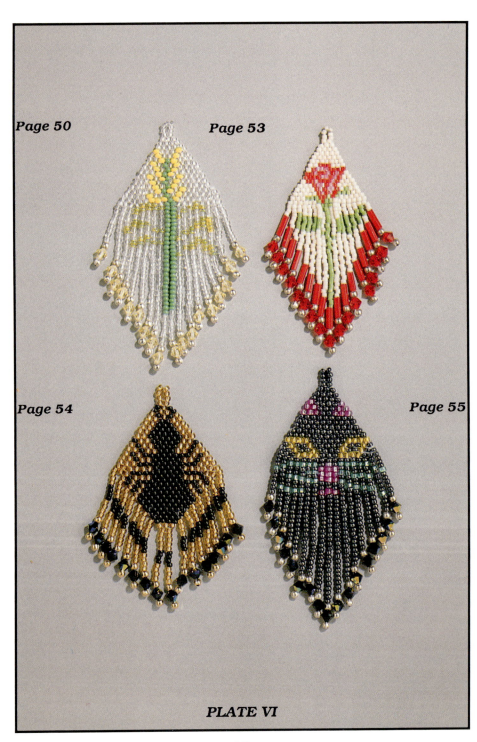

Page 50   Page 53

Page 54   Page 55

PLATE VI

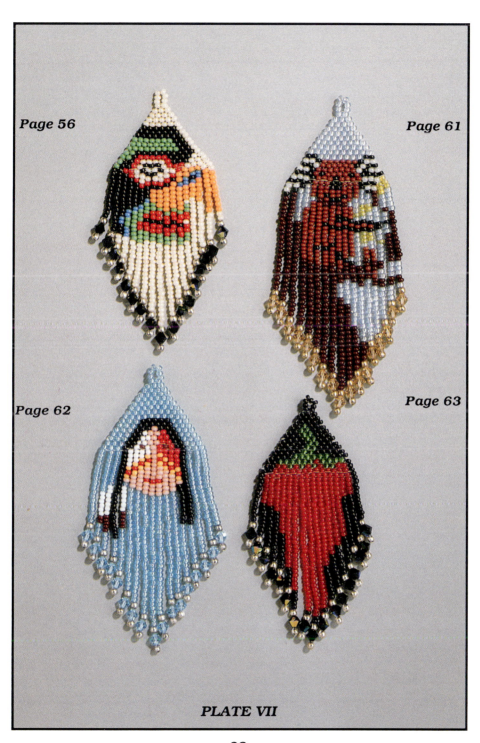

Page 56

Page 61

Page 62

Page 63

PLATE VII

39

Page 66

Page 67

Page 68

Page 69

PLATE VIII

40

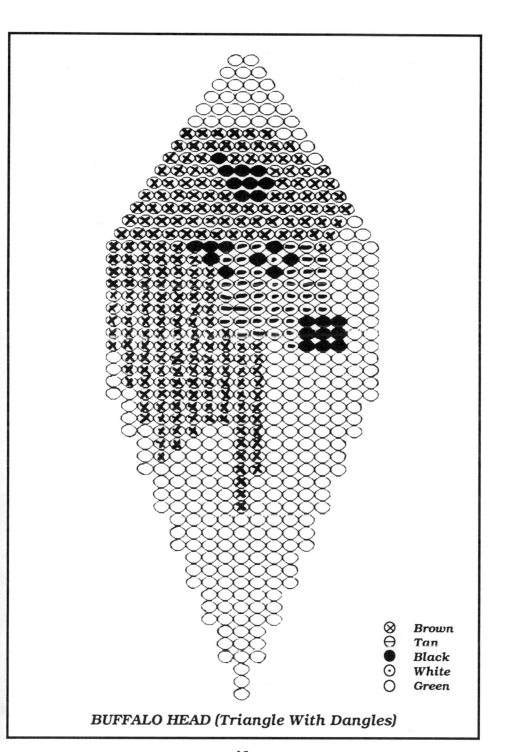

BUFFALO HEAD (Triangle With Dangles)

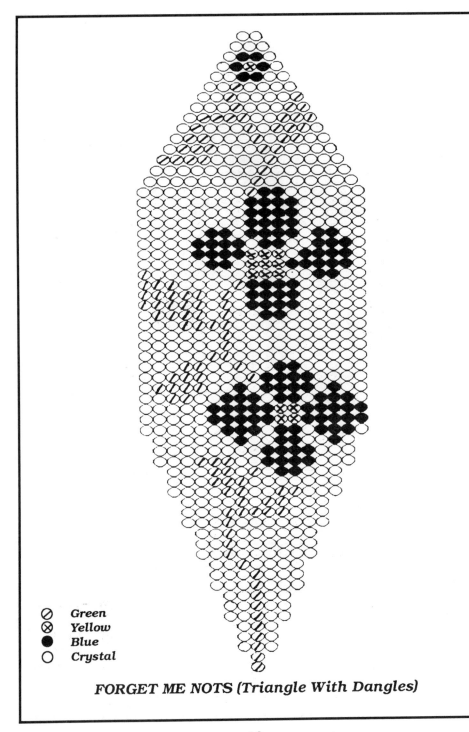

FORGET ME NOTS (Triangle With Dangles)

Green
Yellow
Blue
Crystal

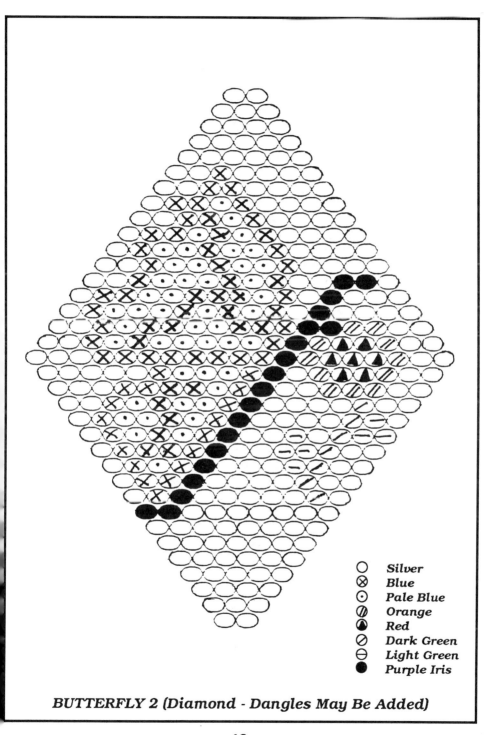

○	Silver
⊗	Blue
⊙	Pale Blue
◍	Orange
◕	Red
⊘	Dark Green
⊖	Light Green
●	Purple Iris

BUTTERFLY 2 (Diamond - Dangles May Be Added)

43

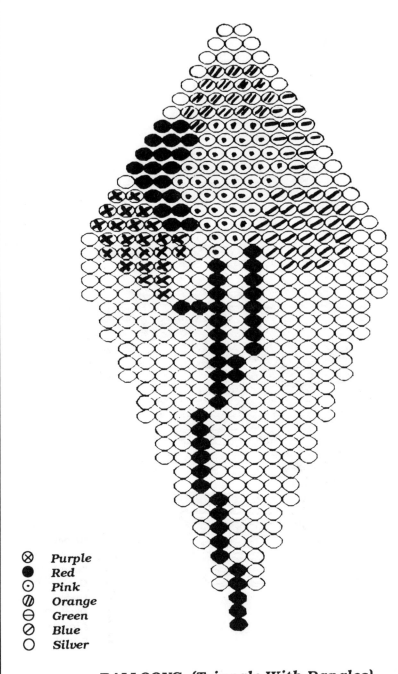

⊗	Purple
●	Red
⊙	Pink
⊘	Orange
⊖	Green
⊘	Blue
○	Silver

BALLOONS (Triangle With Dangles)

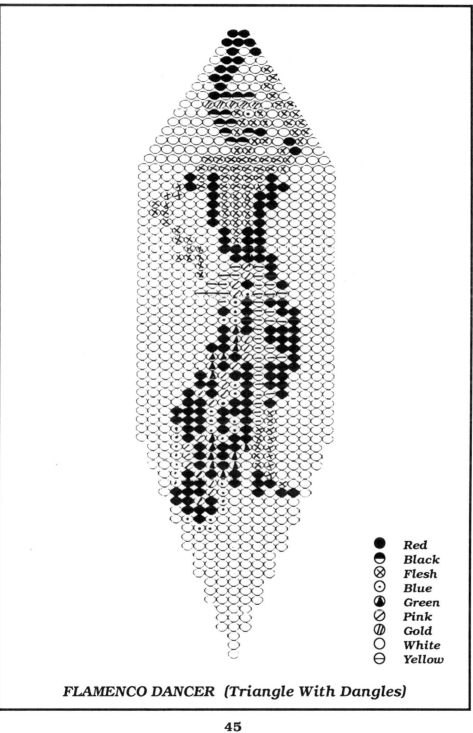

Red
Black
Flesh
Blue
Green
Pink
Gold
White
Yellow

FLAMENCO DANCER (Triangle With Dangles)

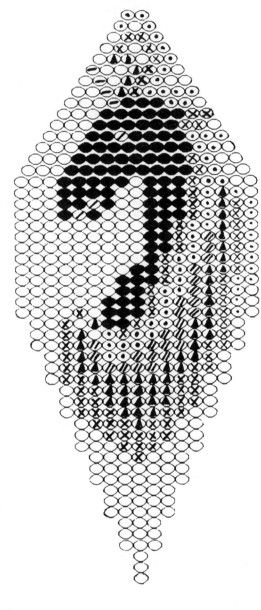

○	Pink
●	White
⊖	Gold
⊙	Purple
⊗	Green
⊘	Black
▲	Yellow
⊘	Pale Pink

UNICORN (Triangle With Dangles)

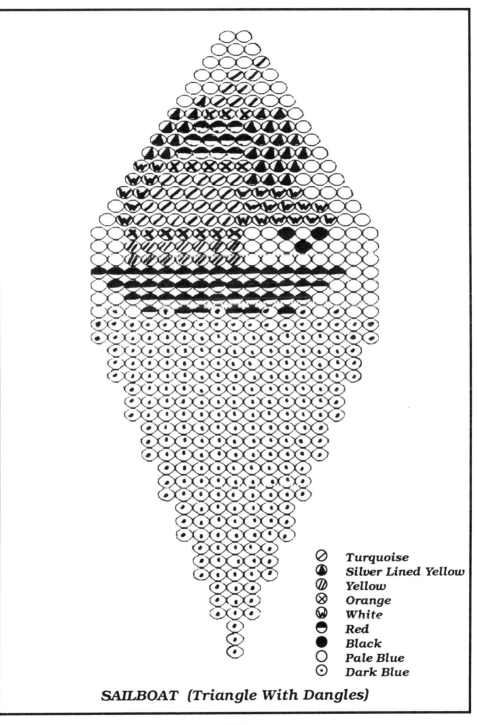

⊘	Turquoise
◕	Silver Lined Yellow
⊘	Yellow
⊗	Orange
⊛	White
⊖	Red
●	Black
○	Pale Blue
⊙	Dark Blue

SAILBOAT (Triangle With Dangles)

47

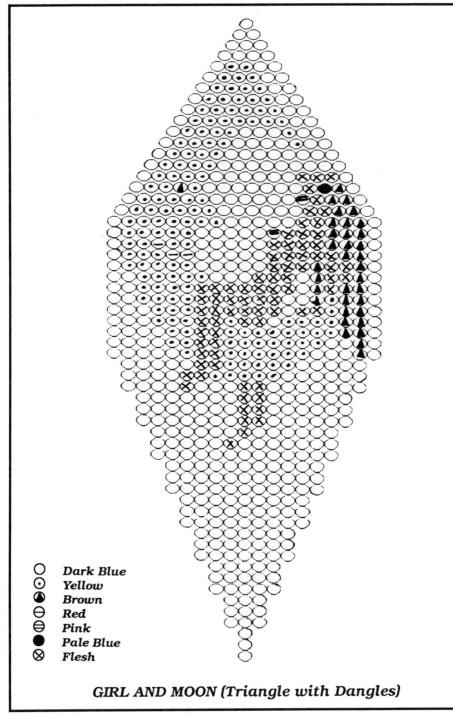

O Dark Blue
⊙ Yellow
◑ Brown
⊖ Red
⊜ Pink
● Pale Blue
⊗ Flesh

GIRL AND MOON (Triangle with Dangles)

48

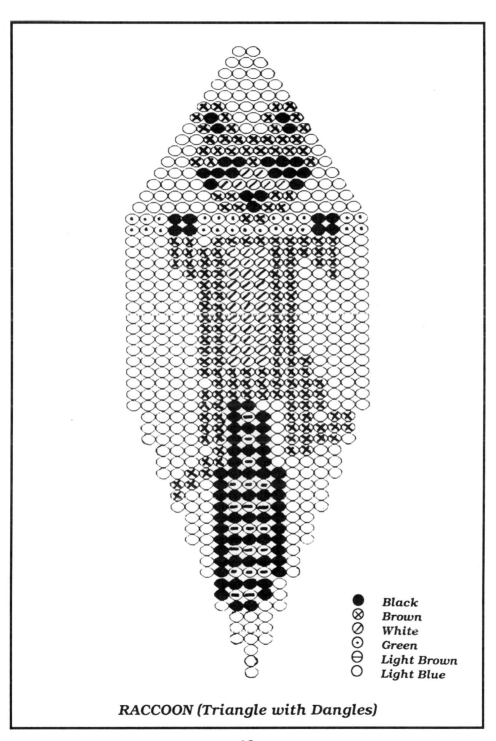

RACCOON (Triangle with Dangles)

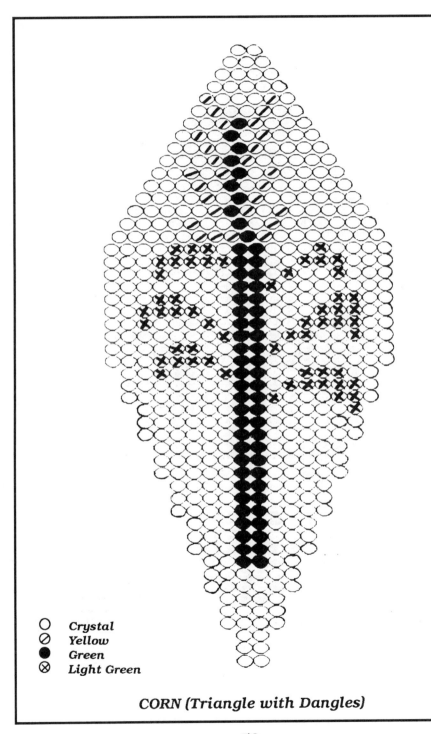

○	*Crystal*
⊘	*Yellow*
●	*Green*
⊗	*Light Green*

CORN (Triangle with Dangles)

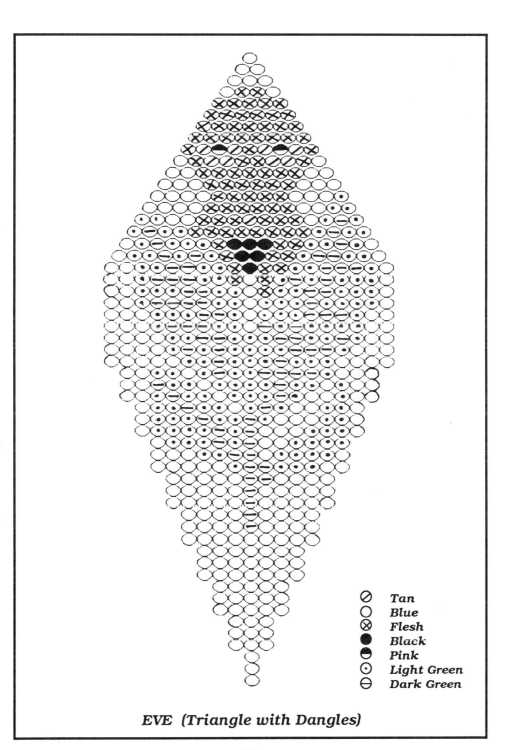

⊘	*Tan*
○	*Blue*
⊗	*Flesh*
●	*Black*
⊖	*Pink*
⊙	*Light Green*
⊖	*Dark Green*

EVE (Triangle with Dangles)

51

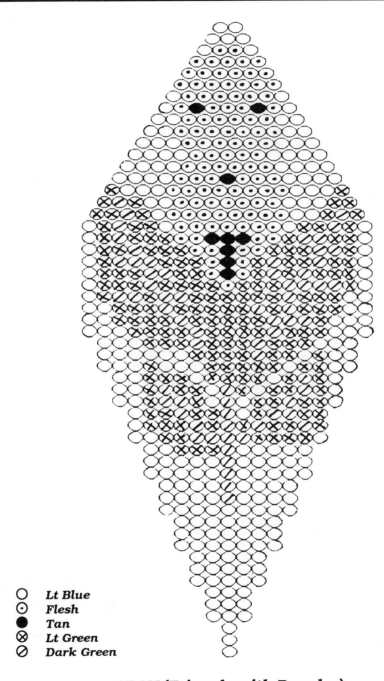

ADAM (Triangle with Dangles)

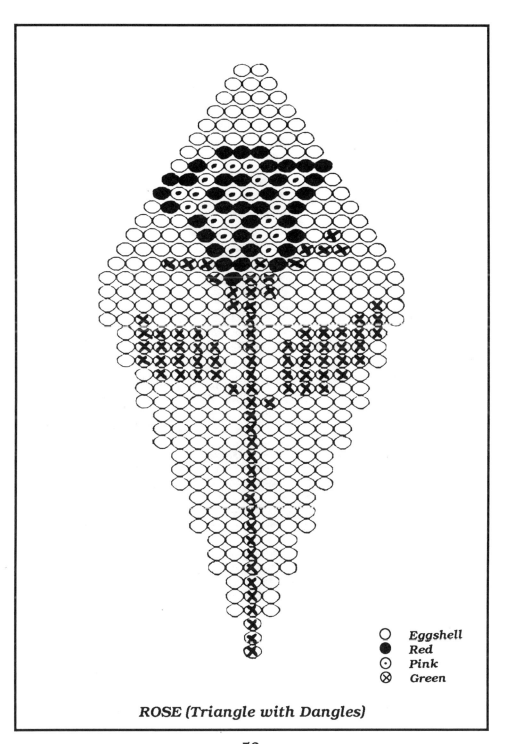

ROSE (Triangle with Dangles)

Legend:
- ○ Eggshell
- ● Red
- ⊙ Pink
- ⊗ Green

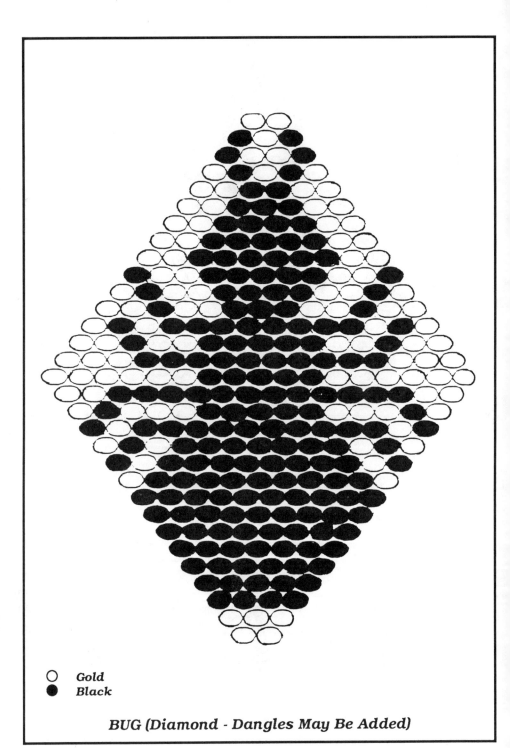

O *Gold*
● *Black*

BUG (Diamond - Dangles May Be Added)

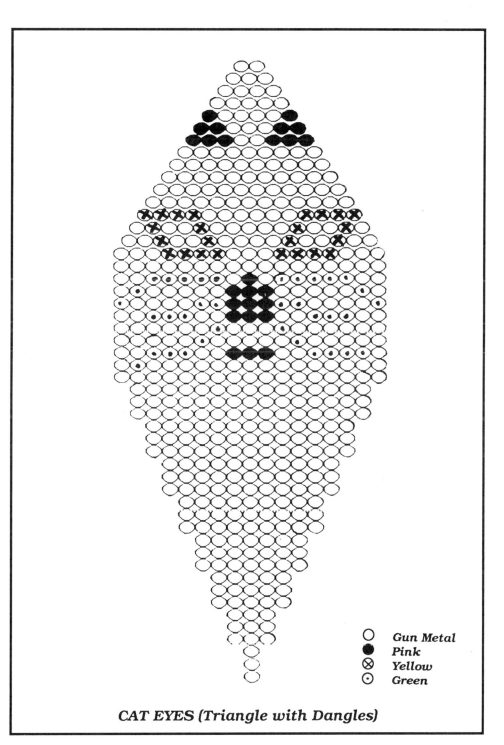

CAT EYES (Triangle with Dangles)

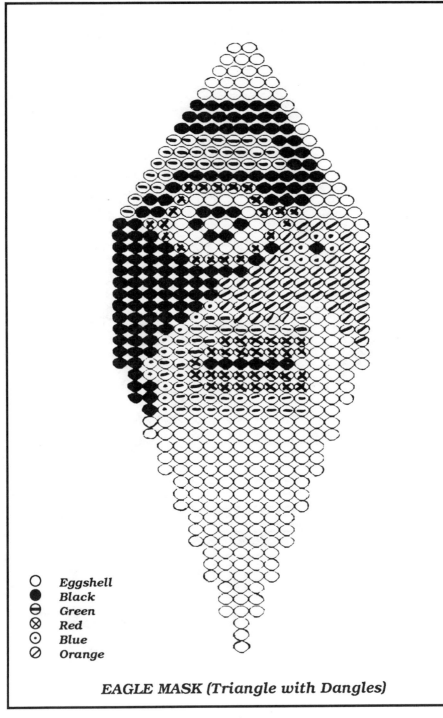

Eggshell
Black
Green
Red
Blue
Orange

EAGLE MASK (Triangle with Dangles)

56

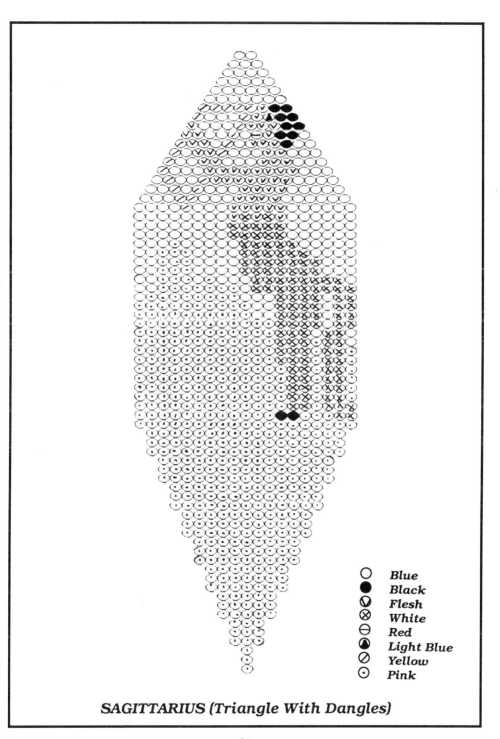

○	Blue
●	Black
◑	Flesh
⊗	White
⊖	Red
◓	Light Blue
⊘	Yellow
⊙	Pink

SAGITTARIUS (Triangle With Dangles)

57

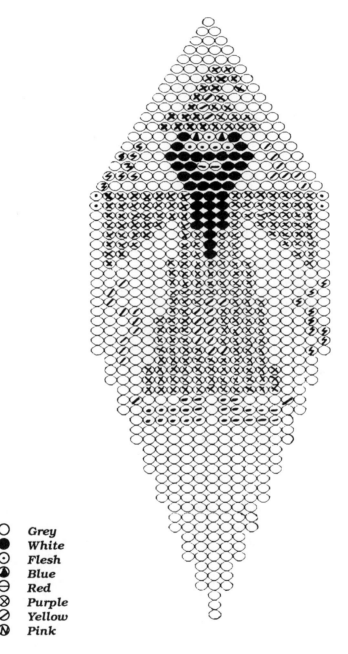

O	Grey
●	White
⊙	Flesh
◓	Blue
⊖	Red
⊗	Purple
⊘	Yellow
Ⓝ	Pink

MERLIN (Triangle with Dangles)

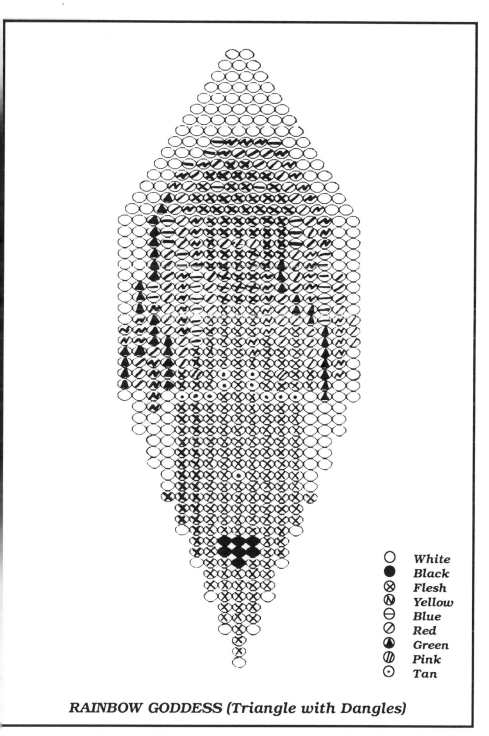

RAINBOW GODDESS (Triangle with Dangles)

○	White
●	Black
⊗	Flesh
Ⓝ	Yellow
⊖	Blue
⊘	Red
▲	Green
⬧	Pink
⊙	Tan

59

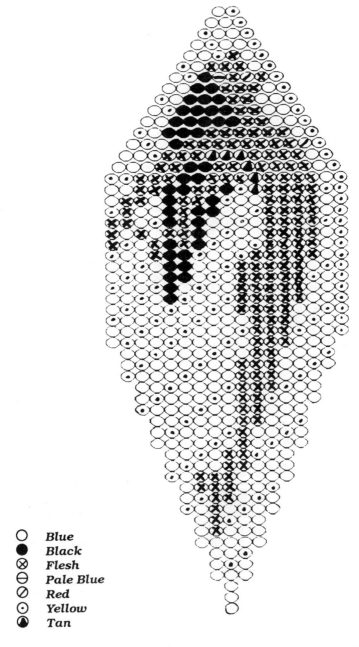

○ Blue
● Black
⊗ Flesh
⊖ Pale Blue
⊘ Red
⊙ Yellow
◕ Tan

SUN GODDESS (Triangle with Dangles)

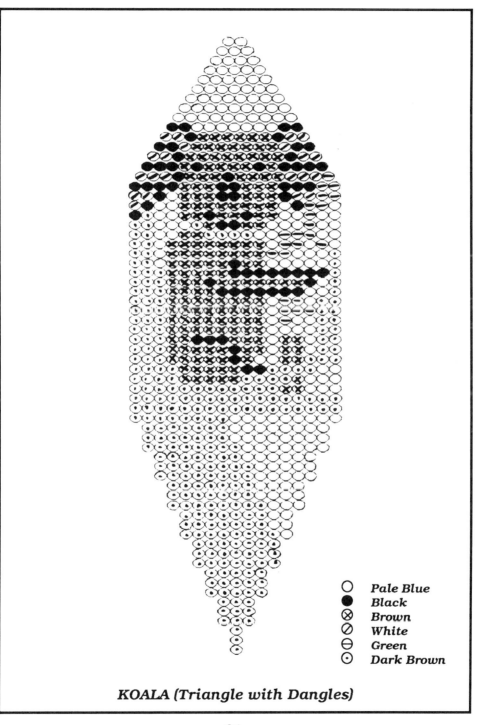

○	Pale Blue
●	Black
⊗	Brown
⊘	White
⊖	Green
⊙	Dark Brown

KOALA (Triangle with Dangles)

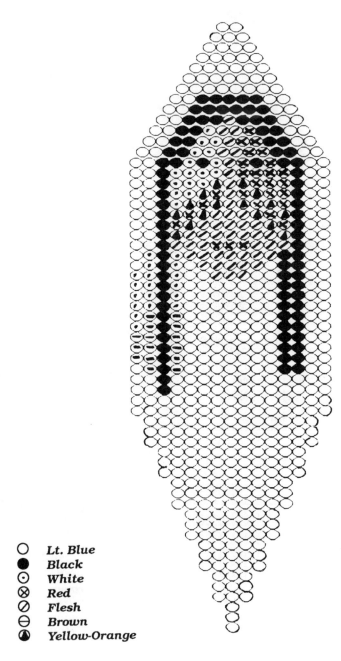

SHAMAN (Triangle with Dangles)

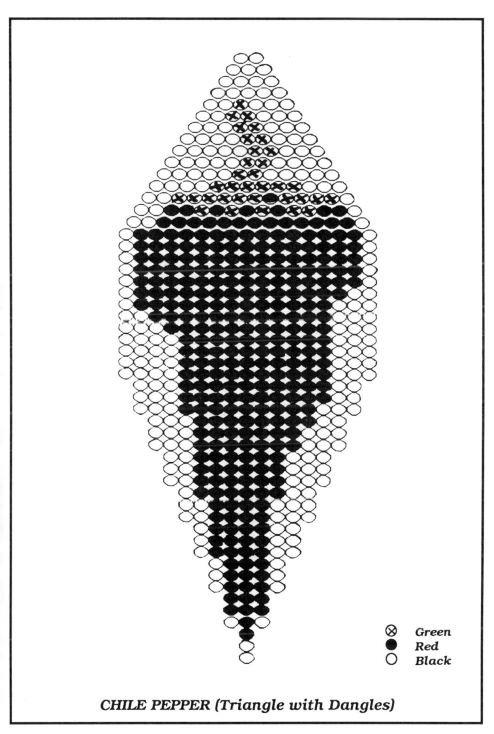

⊗	Green
●	Red
○	Black

CHILE PEPPER (Triangle with Dangles)

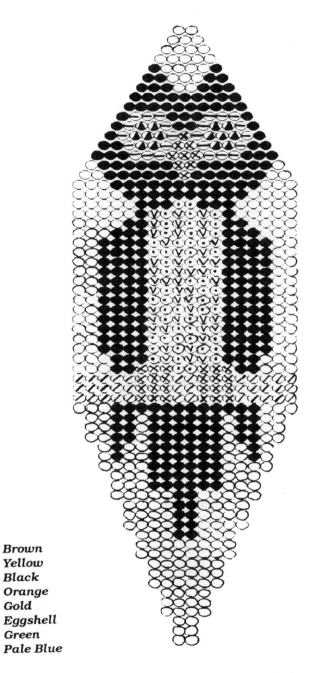

●	Brown
⊖	Yellow
◉	Black
⊗	Orange
Ⓥ	Gold
⊙	Eggshell
⊘	Green
○	Pale Blue

OWL (Triangle with Dangles)

64

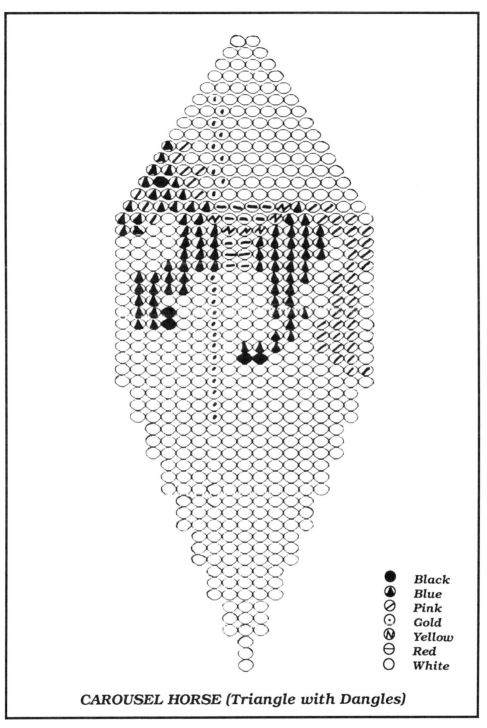

Black
Blue
Pink
Gold
Yellow
Red
White

CAROUSEL HORSE (Triangle with Dangles)

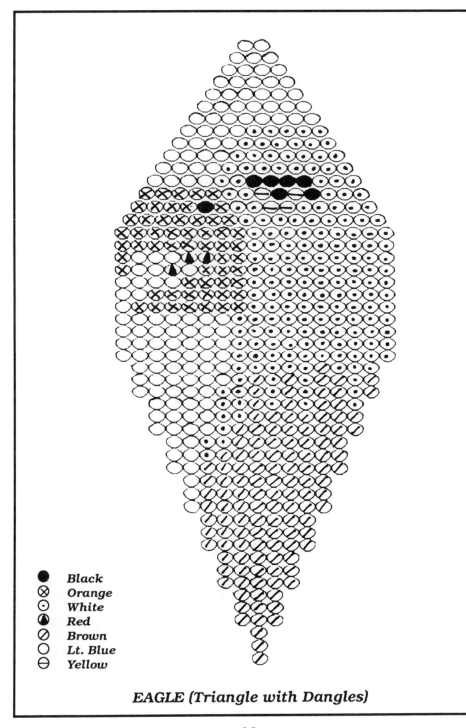

Symbol	Color
●	Black
⊗	Orange
⊙	White
◓	Red
⊘	Brown
○	Lt. Blue
⊖	Yellow

EAGLE (Triangle with Dangles)

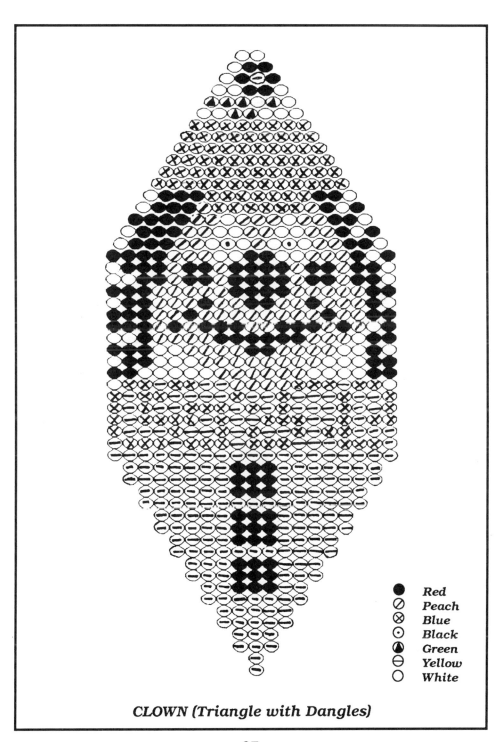

CLOWN (Triangle with Dangles)

67

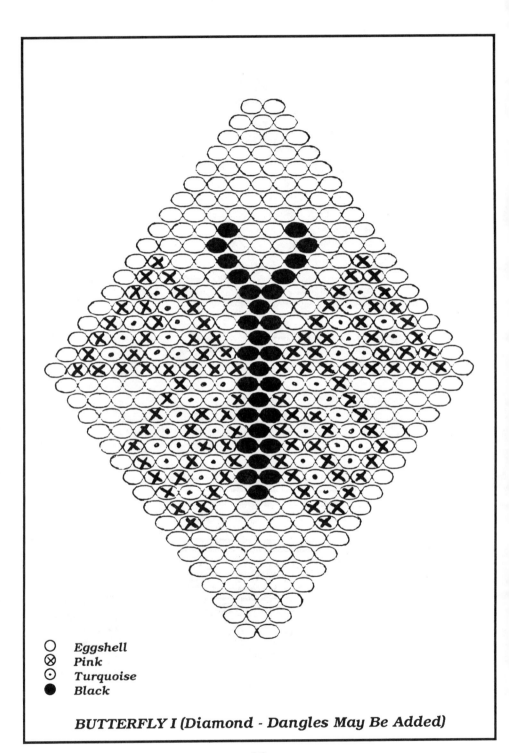

O Eggshell
⊗ Pink
⊙ Turquoise
● Black

BUTTERFLY I (Diamond - Dangles May Be Added)

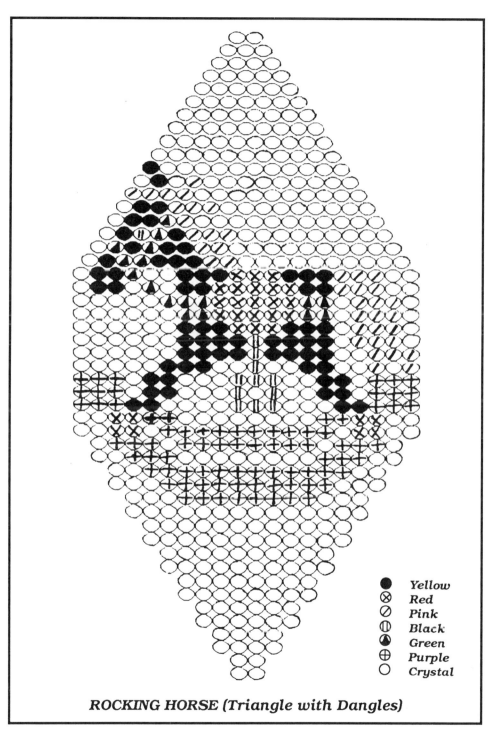

ROCKING HORSE (Triangle with Dangles)

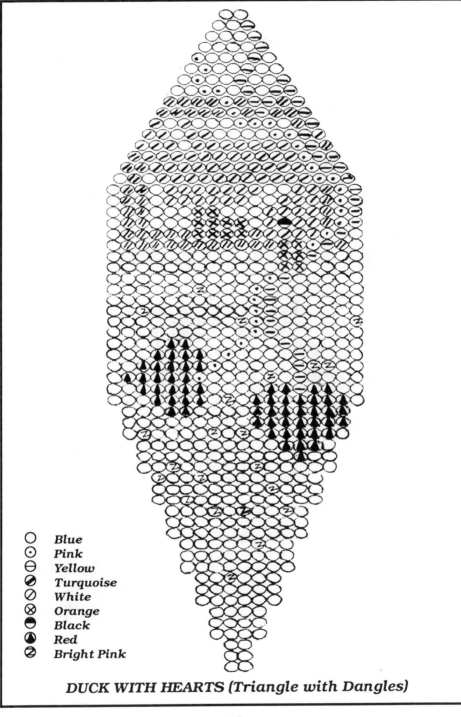

O Blue
⊙ Pink
⊖ Yellow
⊘ Turquoise
⊘ White
⊗ Orange
● Black
◗ Red
∅ Bright Pink

DUCK WITH HEARTS (Triangle with Dangles)

SOME EAGLE'S VIEW PUBLISHING
BEST SELLERS THAT MAY BE OF INTEREST:

The Technique of Porcupine Quill Decoration
  Among the Indians of North America
    by William C. Orchard (B00/01) $8.95
        In Hardback (B99/01) $15.95
The Technique of North American Indian
    Beadwork by Monte Smith (B00/02) $10.95
        In Hardback (B99/02) $15.95
Techniques of Beading Earrings by Deon
    DeLange (B00/03) $7.95
More Techniques of Beading Earrings
    by Deon DeLange (B00/04) $8.95
America's *First* First World War: The French
    and Indian War by Tim Todish (B00/05) $8.95
Crow Indian Beadwork by Wildschut &
    Ewers (B00/06) $8.95
New Adventures in Beading Earrings by
    Laura Reid (B00/07) $8.95
North American Indian Burial Customs by
    Dr. H. C. Yarrow (B00/09) $9.95
Traditional Indian Crafts by Monte Smith
    (B00/10) $8.95
Traditional Indian Bead and Leather Crafts
    by M. Smith & M. VanSickle (B00/11) $9.95
Indian Clothing of the Great Lakes: 1740-1840
    by Sheryl Hartman (B00/12) $10.95
        In Hardback (B99/12) $15.95
Shinin' Trails: A Possibles Bag of Fur Trade
    Trivia by John Legg (B00/13) $7.95
Adventures in Creating Earrings by Laura Reid
    (B00/14) $9.95
A Circle of Power by William Higbie (B00/15) $7.95
        In Hardback (B99/15) $13.95
Etienne Provost: Man of the Mountains by
    Jack Tykal (B00/16) $9.95
        In Hardback (B99/16) $15.95

<<<<< >>>>>